BEING

Conversations with
Florian Schlosser

NON-DUALITY PRESS

First published 2006
by 220 Publishing
PO Box 220, Harrow, HA3 5SW
www.twotwentypublishing.com

Published July 2009 in North America
by Non-Duality Press,
PO Box 2228, Salisbury, SP2 2GZ
www.non-dualitypress.com

ISBN 978-0-9563091-1-2

Florian Schlosser's website is
www.florianschlosser.com

The following people kindly read
the proofs and made valuable
comments:

Kiran Coelho
Gina Holland
Dorian Schultz
Stephen Thomas
Rick Trask
Ingrid Zimmermann
Julia Zimmermann

TO THE LOVE OF TRUTH

THE HOLY MOUNTAIN ARUNACHALA, TIRUVANNAMALAI, INDIA

In man's eternal love affair with truth, it is a joy to discover pointers that express our own knowing in a way that is accessible to us. Florian's book, written in a way that is easily understandable and with deep insight, invites the reader to the recognition of what the sages have been pointing to through the ages. Enjoy.

Isaac Shapiro

With my whole heart I embrace all the wonderful people who invaluably contributed to the creation of this book. Thank you to everyone who shared his or her heart, who investigated into truth and who has been available for these meetings of the heart.

In particular I am most grateful to my teacher Isaac Shapiro for his silent, gentle and liberating company throughout the last six years. You are an example and true teacher for me.

My deep appreciation belongs to Jim Whiting, who with loving sensibility and over countless numbers of hours transcribed and edited the recordings. While reading the transcriptions I again and again have been touched by the love for truth that acted through you. Thank you.

Above all I am most grateful to my partner Julia for the love, the strength, the being and the invaluable support that she is for me in all imaginable fields of life. Without you, more than likely these lines would not be written. Thank you.

Florian Tathagata

INVITATION

This is a book about life and the beliefs that separate us from the only time and place where life can be found, beliefs that take us away from simply being. The conversations on which this book is based are mostly from exchanges between Florian Tathagata and participants of a ten-day retreat in southern India in January 2005 near the foot of the holy mountain Arunachala.

In reading the book the invitation is to share in the special energy of the retreat and participate in its investigation of what is true. Some of the questions may seem to apply only to the people asking them, but at the heart of each question is the love that is seeking to express itself more fully and life seeking to free itself from what is untrue. In the replies are words that speak to us all and the book will repay reading more than once.

The mind is constantly tempting us to leave this moment. I am writing this introduction the day before the book needs to be put to bed. Everything else is ready, and before I sat down to write this, the mind was suggesting that I should have done it earlier. It then created a picture of the book launch and how much more enjoyable that might be than making the final arrangements for the book to be sent to the printer. Both suggestions are lies, but it is easy to be taken in by them.

In a unique way of expressing non-duality, Florian Tathagata uses some terms in specific ways and to avoid confusion it may be helpful to have some understanding of these before reading the book. A frequent word is 'contraction'. This describes a tightening up, felt in the body, as a reaction to present experience. By the word 'beingness' what is pointed to is a wakeful inner passivity and stillness that embraces the totality of the present moment. Within this beingness, action arises without 'doing'. The words 'soft' and 'softness' are used to speak of a gentle way of inwardly meeting the actual experience. By 'focusing' is meant concentration of attention and energy on to any thought, feeling, sensation or outer object.

The word 'perfect' refers to present reality prior to any interpretation of it. Another key term in the book is 'not moving'. By this is meant not picking up any thought, feeling or sensation and making it ours; not following any behavioral pattern or habitual reaction. 'Breaking of the heart' refers to gently allowing ourselves to be touched by whatever is at the core of being.

My experience in hearing Florian Tathagata is that my listening is primarily heart centered. If the listening moves to the head, I am gently brought back to the heart and the body. I warmly invite you to join me in this heart centered listening while reading this book. One of the main things I have learned during the times I have spent with Florian is to avoid the tendency to always look for answers and to place more value on the right questions. The book is not designed to add to the mind's store of knowledge, but to encourage an ever-fresh investigation into what works in life and what doesn't. In this inquiry, good questions work for us in a way that answers cannot.

Jim Whiting
Editor

SUBJECTS OF QUESTIONS AND QUOTATIONS

Are you enlightened?   11

Is it true there is no past and no future in reality?   12

I would like to have a way to deal with my thoughts.   14

Very gently receive what shows up in your awareness.   21

There are periods of time when I feel well and free
    and others when everything is completely
    different.   22

I do not feel that I am in harmony or at peace.
    I want to be free.   29

Is any effort needed in changing the focus of attention?   32

Pretty often I feel that if I say no to what another
    person wants from me I am being egoistic.   37

Old stories from the past are coming alive again
    in me.   42

I am having trouble with emotional disturbance
    generated by my thoughts.   43

I want to ask about taking responsibility for patterns.   50

There is a difference between being our feelings
    and having feelings.   52

I have lots of questions about relationships.   53

This moment – now – is as much God as it gets.   62

What is the difference between seeing and projecting? 63

Usually with our mind and with our senses, we try
    to meet the world from the inside out. 69

I am desperately reading Ramana Maharshi's books. 70

Sometimes reality can be too much. 76

Not wanting to be in the body is a big trap. 79

I always seem to project my thoughts into the past
    or future. 80

Being a spiritual person is opposed to being awake. 85

At one point in my life I learned that my mother had
    not wanted me to be born. 86

Last night a very painful insecurity was coming up. 90

Can you meet emotional pain without wanting
    someone to hold you? 92

Truth is not interested in personality 93

There are things that happened in the past between
    my son and his father. 94

I feel a sense of 'I am' and a connectedness, but . . . 96

How can I live as the love that I am? 99

I was touched by the question
    'How can I live as love?'. 102

*On the pages that follow, the initial question of a conversation is
shown in blue italics and supplementary questions in black italics*

Only when we can
meet things without
wanting them to change
can this world change
dramatically.

There are so many
things in the world that
just want to be met
as they are.

Are you enlightened?

Who is enlightened? Who wakes up? There is no-one who wakes up; there is simply a shift of attention that brings about a recognition that as long as the focus of attention is turned towards objects there is a sense of me, and in the shift of attention to awareness itself that sense of me disappears. That sense of me is a little movement of not wanting to experience what is being experienced now or of commenting on or interpreting the experience that is being experienced now. This sense of me has no real existence. There is awareness and in this the present moment appears. Separation between awareness and the moment has no reality and when the movement of separation comes home it is seen that there is nobody there. All there is is awareness in which life happens.

It is becoming someone having an experience that creates the false separation between awareness and the experience. The trap is to believe that enlightenment is an experience; all that happens is the disappearance of the false experiencer between experience and awareness. Never claim anything. Awareness is completely impersonal.

Is it true there is no past and no future in reality?

Yes. There is only past and future when you believe your thoughts to be reality. Without the belief in them, time does not exist.

So if I don't think, I am here?

And you are here also when you think. In truth it is not you thinking. Thinking thinks. And it is not you who feels. Feeling feels. And it is not 'I am'. Being is. It all has nothing to do with us; not even that awareness has anything to do with us – it is not 'I am aware'. Awareness is aware. It has absolutely nothing to do with you or me or anybody else. Only when we refer anything to ourselves does it become 'your experience' or 'my experience'.

Labelling can happen and thinking can happen if we don't believe in it. If we do not believe it has anything to do with reality, then we are fresh even amidst thinking or unpleasant feelings. When we speak about something called the ego we are actually speaking about something that does not exist; it is only a subtle movement of not wanting to have the experience we are having right now or wanting another experience that we like. If we do not label that subtle sense of I, we will not find much, simply a contraction. Can you meet that contraction without giving it a name? Because it has no reality; it has no substance.

That's what they call illusion?

Yes, but I don't even like the word illusion. 'Illusion', 'ego', 'the self' have been interpreted so much that we started to believe in the interpretations of other people. Do not believe in anyone's interpretation, however beautiful the teaching may be. Forget it, just look for yourself.

We can play with language or speech because it can clear things up for us, but that very seeing itself has nothing to do with speech, thought or feeling; it is independent of these. It is unsensational. For some years, when people asked me a question about reality I did not like to answer them, because it felt like describing it was making more out of it than it is. It is so subtle, that any word about it is too much. Words can only be a pointer.

I have been in India for quite a while and have been to different ashrams, but what I am missing is the ability to switch off my thoughts during meditation. I practice different methods of meditation and I try different ways to switch off my thoughts. There are so many impressions and so many new things. I would like to have a way to deal with my thoughts.

So first of all, let us very simply and with no philosophy, no religion and nothing spiritual, just be very ordinary. Let's have a look at how that mechanism of thought functions. In this moment, here now, who is thinking?

Me.

If you were the thinker of your thoughts you would have the capacity to stop them, because if you walk you can stop whenever you want, and if you want to start again, you start again. This is the-nature of being the walker. So now if you are the thinker of your thoughts, please stop your thoughts. Stop thinking and in 20 seconds start again — and in between not even one thought.

But I had a thought.

So I think it is clear that it is not possible for us to stop our thoughts.

Sometimes it is.

Yes, but it is coincidental. Nobody has really any influence on stopping the thoughts. In Buddhism sometimes monks sit in front of a white wall for 20 years trying to stop the thoughts and suddenly they recognise that this is not possible. So thoughts are happening. If you're tired or you do a lot of exercises, usually the amount of thought is reduced because a lot of energy has gone out of the body and is not generating thoughts, but they come back again. So, if you meditate and you calm down the mind you're very lucky because it is having fewer thoughts, but the moment you open your eyes the thoughts come back. That's your experience. That's my experience. So we will not be very successful in trying to stop thoughts. Thoughts are coming and going, endlessly.

It is the same with feelings and emotions. Let us have a look at these. Who is the feeler of the feelings and emotions? They're moving and they change, but do you control them? No. Now let us have a look at the sensations of the body, like cold, wet, relaxed, dry, etc. Who is the one who senses these sensations? If you are doing the receiving of sensations, please change what you are receiving in this moment, immediately. Thought, feeling and sensations of the body are just happening without any control on your part. You don't know what is going to be the next thought, you don't know what you'll be feeling tomorrow and your body gets older every second and we cannot stop it. Any attempt to control these will not work. We have tried controlling with different methods, and it definitely does not depend on what you try. Just the attempt to stop these things will sooner or later lead to the point of realisation that it is not possible.

Then why do we do meditation?

Who is the one who is meditating?

I am.

Who is this 'I' or this feeling, this sense of 'I' who sits down on a pillow, closes the eyes and meditates? Who is the one?

I don't know.

That's exactly the right answer. You don't know. You don't know who is sitting there. It feels like you are sitting there but when you very precisely look at it, who is sitting? You don't know. So in this moment now, who is sitting in that chair?

I am sitting here. It is the emotions, the thoughts, the body, the soul, whatever.

That's the normal answer. Now let us look if it is true. You said the 'I' was thought, emotion, body, soul, whatever it is — so let's have a look. At this moment are you aware of the thoughts you are having?

Yes.

You can see them. Everyone can see the thoughts coming and going. So just by the fact that you can see them, it's not possible that you are the thoughts. There must be something that sees the thought, so you are not the thoughts.

OK.

Very good, so now you are getting clear. It is the same with emotions; emotions are coming and you are aware of those emotions and see that the emotions are changing constantly. There is something which is simply aware of the emotion, so you cannot be the emotion. You have emotions, but you are not the emotions. It is the same with the body. Let us have a look. In this moment we all are aware, more or less, of being here in the body, true? We all are aware of the sensations we have. So there is an awareness and there is a body, so you are not the body because you can see and are aware of the moving sensations of the body. You are not your thoughts, you're not feelings and you're not sensations of the body.

Now let us have a look precisely at what it is that is aware. There is something which is aware in this moment, so what is it? What is that awareness. It is prior to all thoughts, prior to all feelings, prior to the body experience. What is that which is aware now?

It is something that is always there but you don't feel it for the very reason it is always there.

Yes, this is you, it's consciousness, it's what you are beyond any self-image — that which is aware of every single movement and every single moment. It has never changed. What changed were the feelings, the experiences. Your feelings have changed countless times like the experience of everyone has changed. That which remained was consciousness; so you — as consciousness — never changed. Whatever you did had no effect on that.

It's the simplest thing in life. It's so close you can easily miss it or dismiss it because it is so very simple. Why? Usually because our attention is on the content of our experience, on thoughts and feelings. When the direction of attention is away from awareness itself, we overlook the truth that awareness is already here. We become focused on trying to change our experience instead of being the awareness. The 180-degree turnaround of attention to awareness is what people call awakening. Our attention turns towards awareness itself instead of being hooked on the experience.

If you want to get rid
of your thoughts it is
guaranteed you will
double the thoughts.
If you want to get rid of pain,
you get double pain.
If you want to get rid of
not being enlightened
you will be doubly
unenlightened.

Very gently receive what shows up in awareness. Whatever is revealed in that awareness, I invite you from the heart not to involve the mind. Some places in you would love to be met: places in which you do not feel yourself when they pop up. You do not feel safe in meeting them, and so long as you do not feel safe in meeting them, other people will have a feeling of tension when they meet you, and I know you do not want that. The moment you meet these unfamiliar places in you and allow them to be fully experienced, you can allow yourself to be yourself amidst them. That will have a huge effect on the way you can meet other people and how other people feel with you when you meet them. So I invite you to very softly be with whatever shows up and fully meet the actual sensation which drives it.

There are periods of time when I feel well and free and there are periods of time when everything is completely different. Right now I have the impression that there is something like an explosion in my head.

For most of us the experience you describe is daily life. Sometimes we feel well; the next moment something comes up to disturb this and the body contracts. We relax again and then the next thing shows up. For most of us there is a mechanism going on with our attention that we are not even aware of. The moment a contraction happens, all our attention starts focusing on it and we try to get rid of it, repair it or understand it. With this focusing on our sensation, we immediately exclude the rest of life. Suddenly our life consists only of the sensation and a feeling of 'I' focusing on it, like tunnel vision. One end of the tunnel is the feeling of 'I' and at the other end is the sensation we want to get rid of, get away from. It feels pretty narrow, but it's the usual way we human beings deal with unpleasant sensations. We have become so used to this that we are usually not even aware of it.

This mechanism is mostly automatic and nothing will change unless we see the engine behind it. So what drives it? There is a sensation in the body that is not comfortable — let's call it a contraction. Every human drama consists of a contraction in the body and a trying to get away from it. We call it suffering. We try to move away from it at any cost, searching for an exit. So what drives this mechanism of searching for an exit?

It's fear.

What is underneath this fear? What is the fear an interpretation of?

Of something unknown?

What thing unknown?

For example, the future?

What, very precisely, is underneath this fear?

'I'm not good enough'.

That is a thought. So what is underneath? Forget any philosophy or psychology you've ever read. Really investigate what is underneath.

Nothing.

Yes – you cannot find anything; that is right. There is nothing. The only thing you can find is that somewhere in the body there is a contraction. The mind's interpretation is just a labelling of this contraction, and this labelling divides our experience into good and bad. It splits our experience into wanting and not wanting. That's normal human life: subtle contractions in the body and trying to get away from them.

Let's find this point beneath the contraction where nothing has to change. Let us be present in the midst of the actual experience in the body, very softly and tenderly, without trying to change it. How is it if it is allowed to move freely within you?

What do you find when you are having an experience and you don't want to have it? Does it go away? Does it get worse? It can take only a few seconds before you are in hell, a hell that is home made. It isn't given by God, nor by a guru, nor by your partner or your karma – nothing creates it but you. It is just a little movement within your system; a subtle movement we normally don't see.

We only see and feel the result, so there is a constant focusing on the experience we are having — and on how we can get a better one.

This way of using the capacity for giving attention is driven by resistance. Not resistance to something in particular, just a generalized wanting to have what we want and trying to avoid what we don't want. So we live in a mode of being in frequent arguments with God: 'Oh, God, you have made a mistake with this experience I am having at the moment — a big mistake, so please change it'. If we get really depressed we can say: 'God, I can prove to you that you are making a mistake because every experience you have sent me has been the wrong one'.

So now let's have a look to see if there is any possibility of playing with this wonderful capacity for attention in a different way. Try to get a feeling of where the attention is resting. Is it focused on these words, the birds singing or other noises, or is it focused on a feeling within your body?

Well, it changed. At the beginning it was on me and then it expanded to take in everything around.

So the attention is now aware of many sensations simultaneously.

And it continues to expand.

So how is this? Not having the attention trapped, but being the space for everything right now?

It's good.

Now, if we have an experience of freedom without looking into the mechanism by which we again make ourselves unfree, we constantly depend on certain circumstances or people who help us or support us, or whatever. There is a difference between having an experience of freedom and living as freedom. It's a huge difference. You can have many experiences of freedom and love, and in one second the door closes again. To live as freedom — as an embodiment of freedom — within our usual day-to-day circumstances; our family, our work, wherever we live, let's talk about that.

This space in which experience happens now, what exactly is it? Any experience you are having right now, you are aware of. This awareness is here, now,

true? From moment to moment there is awareness of changing experiences. Now, for 30
seconds, be only that awareness – not focused on
the content of awareness but be the awareness,
so that attention is one with the awareness. It is a
180-degree turnaround of attention away from
content to that which is aware of content.

How is it?

*Every time the attention goes to an idea that this
simple awareness seems good, it is gone.*

It is perfect that you see that. So for this moment
let us just be that awareness. We already are it in
truth; it's just a manner of speaking. Let us just
be aware of every experience happening at this
moment, from moment to moment. (Pause . . .)
It is very difficult to describe now isn't it?

Every time I come close there is something in between.

And you are also aware of this mechanism, otherwise you could not talk about it. So now be that
awareness without wanting to change the mechanism. There is really nothing else: it is a matter

of the way we relate to what is appearing. If you just let be what is already here, you are instantly free. It is freedom from moment to moment to moment, allowing what is already in awareness to be here.

You see very clearly now, so instead of trying to store this clarity let it go, let it go immediately. Then it can renew itself next time your body contracts, instead of coming from memory. Then it is always fresh; then there is no risk of it becoming a philosophy or a technique or a therapy – this is none of these; it is seeing freshly the way we function. Then we find that we love to be the space for its own sake, not because we are trying to gain something.

I do not feel that I am in harmony or at peace. I want to be free.

Can you feel yourself under pressure to be more at peace than you are; to be more in harmony than you are?

Yes.

Just feel that pressure as the sensations in the body — without wanting to change it in any way. Just embrace the pressure.

Let the attention drop deeper into the body, including all of the body in the awareness. Very gently, let the attention drop deeper into the body so that there is awareness of every sensation in the body at the same time — all sensations that are happening right now.

Wherever you feel some tension, let that tension be included in awareness. If you try to push against the tension with will and effort, how does the tension react?

It becomes stronger.

Yes, it becomes stronger. Pushing and trying to get rid of it makes it worse. The more you want to be free, the more you are bound.

So you are talking about the whole of the body, not just one area?

Yes, all of it – every cell. How is it now?

There is still pain.

Let that pain be here, and experience the pain and all other sensations at the same time, so that the pain is just one of unlimited sensations happening at this moment.

Only when we focus on the one sensation does the attention become very narrow. Our life becomes concerned only with me and this sensation and how I can deaden it. Open up to all sensations: body sensations, seeing, hearing, thinking, feeling – whatever. The moment we focus, there is immediately a strong sense of two – 'I' and an object – and this creates some effort. That is the fruit of focusing. So just be aware of all the sensations in the body.

Now I feel as though I am trying to expand.

It is a very intense habit that is trying to control your experience. So even in this moment of expansion, there is a trying to 'do it' and this trying is in fact an attempt to control it. That control is trying not to experience all the sensations in your body; when the attention moves to an area of the body that is uncomfortable, this control mechanism steps in.

I feel stuck there.

Feeling stuck is still trying to get out of it. Instead of focusing on the tension, just allow the attention to return into the body. I am not saying bring the attention back to the body — that would be doing the movement of attention and it would not work — but let the attention softly drop into the body. Hold yourself, like a loving father holds his son. No fighting anymore; just holding and loving. You become the father of all sensations, holding them without wanting to change them.

Is any effort needed in changing the focus of attention towards awareness?

Either we focus on an object freely or by reflex. If we don't want something we move away from it and try to focus on something we like instead. So all this is a game of wanting and not wanting. True? Have a look.

Now, instead of seeing where the focus goes, watch what drives the focus. We are not used to looking at what drives it, we are just gaining the fruits and suddenly we are focused on one thing and then we are focused on another. We are constantly the reaction of our focusing but we are not aware of what drives it. Very softly investigate this process of moving; not the object to which it moves, just see that the attention moves. In this moment is there any effort involved in letting the attention move freely?

No.

So there's no need to focus on something; the attention just moves freely. Now go a step further. What is that which is aware of the movement of attention? Something is aware of it otherwise we could not recognise it.

It's the same thing . . .

It's awareness, it's consciousness. So in order to be that consciousness which is already here, do you have to focus anywhere? Does it have any effect on consciousness, does consciousness like or dislike, where the focus of attention is in this moment? No. Consciousness is there and that consciousness, that awareness, is just aware of the moving attention. So attention and consciousness, what is their relationship?

It feels like attention is the spotlight within consciousness.

Yes, and the spotlight can move without being caught on an object. So what is that which sees the focus and which is aware of the focusing?

Space.

Space. The focusing happens within the space. So even if you focus very precisely on an object or a thought or a question, as you need to at times, the space is still there. Attention is a movement and awareness is a space in which this movement happens. Attention on an object has no effect on space. We constantly focus on how I feel, what I think, how the body is. In this moment, who is the one who is aware of whatever you feel, whatever you think, whatever you experience right now? It's not important what you experience. Who or what is aware? See how this question works.

This question is itself a turnaround of attention. This question moves your attention from the content to the space in which content happens. Just this question. Do you have to change anything? Nothing. The moment we are concentrated on something in particular, attention is always narrow, it gets tight. We exclude the rest of the world and it's only about that something and me and how we can deal with it. This is the result. These are the fruits we gain. Ask this question, softly – the secret is softly – Who is the one who is aware? This brings back the attention towards awareness itself. Attention merges with awareness again and the fruit we gain is expansion, an immediate expansion.

I don't know why this question works, I only know that it has a tremendous effect. I always used to think it was about getting the right answer, but that's not true. It is about finding the right question. There are some good questions and they-work by themselves. They work for us. Those questions serve us. The attention is merged with awareness in which there are no fixed answers, and this means a huge expansion — vastness, unlimited vastness.

I always wanted
to know everything,
but there are
secrets about life
I honour so much
that I am not
interested in finding
answers. I just
enjoy what happens,
for this is an
honouring of
innocence.

Pretty often I feel that if I say no to what another person wants from me, I am being egoistic.

I know what you mean, but there is a nuance here we can speak about. If we say no because we think somebody is doing wrong, and we think we know what is right, there is a huge separation: somebody who knows and somebody who does not know; a good guy and a bad guy. Most of the no's are spoken from that belief that something is wrong. Either the other person is wrong or we think we are wrong, and this causes this feeling of egoism.

Sometimes I can be quite tricky in this — I try to force the other one to take the decision to say no.

Does it work?

Most of the time.

What is the cost?

That I feel egoistic, selfish.

Yes, so you know how you create this feeling.

But I get what I want.

No. Because this is not what you want – you don't want to feel that way.

The feeling is not what I want, that's right.

So it doesn't work. Actually you are paying a huge price, and it's good that you see this, because up to now you have really believed that you get what you want in these situations. Now you see you don't get what you want. And in order to cover up the unwanted feeling you do certain things to avoid it, which cause even more feelings that you do not want. Up-to now you did not know how to handle it in a different way, so you just took what was available to avoid the feeling for a time, but after that you felt worse afterwards.

I acknowledge that I have made a decision to live this way and I accept the consequences.

No, that is trying to avoid the feeling; in wilfully accepting it you are actually suppressing it. You are carrying it around all the time. What are you doing to yourself to suppress it?

I drink.

Yes. That's the way you suppress it. Others smoke, watch TV, are sex addicted or addicted to spiritual seeking. It is all exactly the same thing. It is trying to escape this feeling of unhappiness, of not feeling good. You always have to make effort. The moment you stop the effort of acceptance or of running, it shows up. It is always waiting to show up. This effort 'I have to drink', 'I have to accept', 'I have to want' creates tremendous pressure in you.

If I give up the effort I feel a tremendous insecurity.

Can you feel that insecurity now? And when I say feel it I mean the actual sensation in the body. It may be very unfamiliar to meet the sensation, but please try your best.

There is a sort of vibrating in the belly. I am holding my legs to stop them shaking. I would like to let go but I am afraid of losing myself.

Where is the sensation of being afraid to lose yourself?

In the belly and in the legs.

Now very softly meet those sensations. Very softly we are investigating those sensations; not changing, just exploring.

There is a knot in my belly.

Just allow that knot to be here.

It's getting tighter and looser, tighter and looser and I can't control it. That's an uncomfortable feeling for me.

Could you allow that feeling to be here without wanting to control it?

Yes, I could.

Now, will you allow that? Yes or no. It is already there, so will you allow it? And just very tenderly feel it. Don't control it. No need to control your breath; that's an old habit. Now will you allow that knot to be here?

No.

OK, if you don't allow it, what is the price you have to pay? Have a very precise look at the cost.

I paralyze myself.

Yes, if you don't experience that knot you have to paralyze yourself for the rest of your life. Any other costs? Or is that enough?

I think there are a few more costs. One is that I have to control.

Good to see. What else?

It's hard to show myself.

Yes, you always have to hide, so that nobody sees that. You have to keep a sense of separation alive. A huge cost, my friend. Is that enough, or do you still want some other costs? It's good to see the costs.

Actually, I do not want to pay this price.

Yes, I know. But you have never looked before at how the price is generated.

Old stories from the past are coming alive again in me.

They never died. They have always been alive.

They give a bad feeling; 'I haven't had a good life'.

If they are not seen they become very angry, and they start to stink. They become our enemies. But if they are seen, they turn into friends, they start to have a nice fragrance and they turn into wisdom. That's the beauty about old stories. What they need is that they are seen; that we meet them and that we embrace them and honour them. Then they turn into wisdom. Otherwise they are our enemies. That's the beauty about our past. It is not about denying the past or the particular history we went through. It's there in every cell, not divisible from that very being. Without that you will never live in peace. If you live as a guru and pretend you have renounced everything, you haven't. It's in the cells. Use those friends, those old stories; they turn you into a wise man when you love them. That is their gift to you. To be a saint you have to have the blessing of the Pope. And you have to be dead. To me, to be a fully alive ordinary human being is the utmost bliss.

I am having trouble with emotional disturbance generated by my thoughts.

How is it now to be here? Feel the sensations in the body. Just tune into the sensations in the body for a moment – not digging for something or searching for something but seeing the sensations that are already here.

There is a little bit of tightening.

What do you feel?

Right now, a tornado.

Where in the body do you feel this?

Right here (pointing to stomach).

So when you give attention to the sensation, the energy drops from the head to the feeling in the body. So those two questions might be of value to you, when you see that the mind is spinning, just ask yourself these questions 'What do I feel? Where in the body do I feel this?'. And observe what these questions do or show up.

An emotional mess.

So the question shows up an emotional mess.
How does that feel in the body? Just be aware of
the sensations in the body. Usually when we meet
other people who are in some way attractive to
us — especially sexually — but with whom we are
not-yet on familiar terms, all our deepest patterns
of self-protecting show up in one instant. Our
entire system remembers. Every cell remembers
every pain. Every experience we have ever had
with the people we have been drawn to comes
up. So we could say that all the unconscious — the
stored story of our life — is held in the body, and
with this intimate meeting it shows up to be met
in consciousness. That has to happen. It can happen in a relationship between man and woman and
it will happen. And it can happen in a relationship
between teacher and disciple — though I don't like
these words. What we don't want to experience
must show up after the honeymoon period. You
have a honeymoon with your partner, you have a
honeymoon with your teacher, you have a honeymoon with your friends, but when the honeymoon
is over the showing up of what is held in the body
must happen. And when it happens, if we do not

know how to deal with it, we either think there is something wrong with the other person or we think there is something wrong with us. We think 'this is not the right relationship'— and we are quickly out of it.

The moment our history shows up, we experience it as contraction and a bunch of emotions, not knowing where they have so quickly come from. And when we don't know how to deal with that, the mind automatically starts to spin and tries to help us to get away from it. That is the mechanism. The moment we meet someone we are attracted to, we are already on the treadmill.

It's silly, isn't it?

I wouldn't label it silly. It is just that we are not used to dealing with those emotions. We meet someone for whom we have affection, love, and yet inwardly we experience it completely differently, as contraction, fear and all the rest of it. These feelings show up simultaneously. How does it feel to see this funny game? Feel, don't think, just feel. Allow yourself to feel in this very moment.

I now see it as funny.

There is an enjoyment in it showing up. It's a blessing that it shows up. We have been carrying it around for years, knowing that it is there. Every time we meet someone attractive it shows up, so we come to a point where we think we had better not meet anyone anymore.

Yes, I came to that point. Then I enjoyed life.

You lie.

I don't lie completely.

OK, just a little bit of truth. But we are not speaking about being half pregnant. Either you're pregnant or you're not pregnant. Either you're happy or you're not happy. Either you're free or you're not free. Half freedom does not exist. So let us speak about being totally happy with what is, and that includes the showing up of old patterns, otherwise you have to live as a celibate.

What do I do with that which drives me to be what I don't want to be?

You can ask two little questions: 'What do I feel?' and 'Where in the body do I feel it?' Then the attention moves to the feelings, which are much quieter than the agitated mind. These two questions help me tremendously. They invite my attention to check. It's not that I do it. It is that the questions softly direct the attention to the emotions or the body. If you like you can go on to ask 'Who is aware of all this?'.

And this question turns the attention towards awareness itself and you completely relax. A good question is much more valuable than a good answer, because a good question does the job for you. You immediately experience what the question does to you. The right questions make a difference; the answers don't. The answer of today is the misleading belief of tomorrow. But a good question survives.

With these questions I feel an expansion.

Yes and it will continue to expand. What expands is your capacity to be present in the actual experience. This is what expands. You can have this expansion on your own quite easily – this is the half-baked buddha. The fully-baked buddha is able to have this expansion in meeting other people also. It's the next stage. Living in a cave is pretty easy after a while. Returning to the game will show up some interesting new patterns, which we may have thought we had already dealt with. No way. This is why I embrace the world so fully. It gives the blessing of meeting myself even more deeply. I spent some time in a monastery and this is why I came out. This is the beauty of meeting somebody. If you meet somebody and you feel attracted to the light, you are definitely also attracted by the patterns; yours and theirs perfectly fit together. They play out.

Most of the time it is only me having the pattern.

No, this idea is a pattern. Most of the time you think it is only you, and for sure you meet some-body who also thinks it's only you. He's already enlightened, so the pattern must be yours alone.

I only know people like that.

That's the patterns playing together. 'It's always me' needs someone who considers himself already free, someone who thinks he doesn't have any patterns anymore. It is an old pattern of yours to take everything on your shoulders. Men love to be the gurus for the women; they love it, and as long as you believe in this old pattern you will be looking for a man who is a guru for you.

I want us both to be gurus.

That takes a while. First become human, then you will see if you both have any interest in becoming gurus.

I want to ask about what you have said about our taking responsibility for our patterns. When patterns arise in me, I say to myself 'I am not the doer'.

This is jumping over – the perfect way to jump over. It is using beingness to avoid facing your patterns.

When you say take responsibility for our patterns, I am not sure what you mean.

The moment a pattern appears it happens only in your body and not another, so it is a very personal thing and your responsibility is to allow yourself to face that pattern: to see what price you are going to pay if you let that pattern rule in your life. All this we can label as being responsible for your own pattern. Being responsible is to meet your pattern in a very mature way, to meet it in the natural authority that you are; it is the ability to respond in a natural way that serves your freedom and that serves your happiness and that serves your ability to meet other people. It's a mature way of being, and I am interested in that mature way of meeting you. And you love it too, otherwise you wouldn't be here.

When a pattern is playing out, we know it. We do not need to know anything about it. We do not need to know the source of it, we do not need to know any philosophy. When a pattern plays out we experience it in the body, and it is also in the body that we are going to pay the price. No matter what philosophy you take on or what you believe, it will not prevent you from experiencing the pattern and it will not prevent you experiencing the cost. We are just dealing with reality. Impersonal awareness is aware of the pattern but the pattern is a very personal thing, which we experience in a very personal way. Do not give your authority to any philosophy or any teaching. Just see and meet your own stuff; this is the end of romantic ideas and sentimentality, of dreaming of some better world.

When you meditate, what do you do?

Nothing. It is just awareness and not believing in whatever shows up. But not believing in what shows up is not the same as avoiding it. It is being with it; it is a meeting in truth. I meet myself in truth. As long as patterns show up I simply meet them without moving.

There is a difference between being our feelings and having feelings. So long as we believe in our interpretations of reality, we *are* our feelings. If we become our feelings, no other possibilities exist for us; the whole world becomes those feelings. When the feelings are brought under observation we *have* feelings; there is a distinction between who we are and the feelings we have.

First, we are the feeling, then we have the feeling. The third stage is to be the space for all feelings, the pure awareness in which all thoughts and feelings come and go without the separation created by being attracted to them, trying to avoid them or trying to manipulate them.

I have lots of questions about relationships.

We all have.

One of the questions I have is about how I often feel that I want to give more affection to other people than they want to receive.

Do you want something from the other?

Yes.

So what do you want when you give more affection than the other person wants?

I want to feel loved or OK.

Does that work?

No.

No, and actually it is manipulation. We give to receive; and if you don't get what you want, what then?

I have to meet the feeling inside me.

Do you meet it? Really meet it? It shows up, sure. Do you really experience how it feels when you don't get what you want?

Not fully, because the pattern continues.

This is a good insight. It will repeat wherever we are, in whatever group of people we are with. It will show up again. Whatever wants to be met will have to show up. I cannot promise anything else.

Thank you.

Some people like to hear that, some people don't. In the lunch break I was speaking with a friend about relationships and I could see I had checked for myself every type of arrangement in our culture, and some outside our culture, to deal with a relationship. Marriage, open relationship, closed relationship, no relationship, being a monk, being on my own, sleeping around. Maybe there are some other options I don't know about, but I have checked all these. The last thing I checked was what I wanted least: to be absolutely fully committed. In the present partnership, a thousand times I have had the impulse to leave or make her

leave. And somehow I didn't leave, and somehow she didn't leave. I cannot foresee the future,
but that very commitment has caused such an
immense pressure in which I could see every
possible justification to leave or make her leave.
But we didn't leave. It is just a willingness to
experience whatever comes up; not to move.
It is a knowing of the truth that leaving or looking
for somebody else will not end the need to face
whatever needs to be faced. And somehow things
have been met inside myself that I could not even
have dreamt of. I could not have had the slightest
idea that those patterns were there.

Sometimes it was hell for me and for her. So when
we speak about relationships – all types of relationship, including friendship, teacher and disciple
– only a few will stay with you long term. As long
as we get what we want, everything is nice. The
moment something shows up that is not comfortable and you are not clear enough to stay, either
you go or you sabotage things to make the other
one leave. Nothing else is possible until we know
about the possibility of living as awareness amidst
the greatest pain. Some say that is the biggest
power in the universe.

How does it feel to speak without illusion, without any promise that there is a realm of endless happiness in a relationship? How does that feel?

It's kind of a relief.

Yes, otherwise you will be on the run for the rest of your life in search of some kind of perfection, or you will be constantly avoiding a relationship. To avoid any deep emotional connection, you can take some magic mushrooms or other drugs. But beingness is not the same thing as a good feeling.

Beingness embraces bad feelings also. So the invitation is not to relieve ourselves of bad feelings, because this is the trap, but to relieve ourselves of having to have a good feeling. Beingness embraces hell when hell is the reality and, in any profound relationship, hell will show up at times.

Do you think it matters who the person is who you go into that deep commitment with?

No.

Just that both are willing.

Not even both. One is enough. Even if you both say you want commitment, each will have a different idea of what commitment means.

You talk about staying, right?

I talk about not moving.

OK, but every time I've left a relationship it has been beneficial. It was much better that it ended.

What was better? You felt better, that is what was better. So as long as you believe you need a good feeling to be with someone, so long as the ground of a relationship is thought and emotions, the ground will change as soon as something is touched in you. If this is the foundation on which we have built our house the house cannot stand.

Sometimes I have had a strong knowing from my belly that I needed to not be in that particular relationship. It felt like an intuition.

Where do you experience intuition?

It feels like a message from deep within me.

And where do you find it; where do you recognise it? Where do you hear that voice?

In my belly.

No.

I don't understand.

When you have a feeling, who is it recognizing the sensation? Do you really meet it or do you interpret that feeling? There is a feeling in the body; if you just meet this feeling without any interpretation, what does the feeling tell you? If there is no interpreting and no labelling, what does the feeling tell you?

Nothing.

Exactly. This sensation is not speaking with you. What you hear is the interpretation you put on to the feeling. You believe in the interpretation and then it feels as though this interpretation tells you something, according to what you like and what you don't like. It is your likes and dislikes that are speaking.

That very sensation you are having in the body right now, let us see who is communicating with whom? Again, does that sensation speak to you when you don't interpret it, when you don't give it a name?

That's not what I am talking about. I am talking about intuition. There's a difference. Sometimes I just suddenly know something.

Is it intuition? If there has been any psychological process before a decision to go, then you are listening to an interpretation of your feelings; trying to get an answer from it about what is right and what is wrong. Now look at those moments when you left your boyfriend or you made him leave. Was it that everything was fine and next morning you woke up clear, with no agitation, and said 'I am leaving'.

No.

No, there have been lots of emotions involved, lots of thoughts, lots of pain, a lot of projection. All this came together and you did not know how to meet these sensations. There was a lot of confusion and the only way you knew how to get out of this confusion was to leave. There was a listening to that, so to say, 'voice'. But there is no voice, because our emotions don't speak to us. We speak to them. In a relationship, knowing does not need any thought or any emotion. In a relationship it knows whether you are living your truth or whether there is a little trick involved. Living your truth means being really willing to face what shows up in you. The trick that stands in the way of this is believing in justifications, believing in the emotions – that they are true – and believing in thoughts. That very knowing knows if you leave because you don't want to experience some patterns in you or if you just leave. If you leave and there is not the slightest residue in you; if you are perfectly clear of emotional stuff with your partner – complete, no blaming, no bitter taste – then you know it is true knowing: that still, small voice that is free of emotion, free of movement. When there is disagreement, when there is a taking up of a position, then there is a trap. If you think about your ex-boyfriends, are you totally complete with them? Are you still friends with them? Do you feel that they did something wrong or that you did something wrong?

Yes, there is some of that.

That shows that there was some not meeting of a pattern. There is nothing wrong about that, but in each relationship, sooner or later, you have experienced the same; and the pattern will return again and again until you face it. You have not seen the pattern, so you believe in it and you move. If we don't move when the emotion pops up, in that very friction between the clarity of not moving and all the pressure to go, charcoal turns into a diamond. If we leave when the pressure shows up, the charcoal remains charcoal. Only because we have such a smart mind and we believe our own justifications, do we leave one relationship believing the next one is going to be better.

This moment — now — is as much God as it gets. It doesn't need thinking about because it is here. It doesn't need thinking about because it is perfect and you do not need thinking about because as awareness you lack nothing and are also perfect.

If you are really present now, can you be unhappy? If you want to be unhappy you have to generate thoughts and emotions and then believe them. Then it is possible to be unhappy.

Nothing has to be better than it is. That is freedom. Trying to be free from what is true now is bondage.

Nothing is required. You do not need anything to be aware of what you are aware of now and to know yourself as that awareness.

What is the difference between seeing and projecting?

It's simple, very simple. The belief that you are seeing something about another person is projecting.
Meeting your own sensations within is seeing.

*So, if I look at my partner and it seems that maybe
he is in a pattern, is this a projection?*

No, because you are not saying that he is in a
pattern, you say he seems to be in one. And for
whom does this seem?

For me.

Yes, so you speak only from your own experience.
There is a sense in you that something might be
going on in your partner. It is a sense in you, and
if you speak like that you speak truth. You look at
your partner and for you it seems like he is hooked
on something. If you go to your partner and say
'You are in a pattern and I see it very clearly
and I will help you because I know what is going
on in you' this is a projection. But if you say 'I
don't know if I am right, but I have a feeling that
something may be going on in you that you have

become used to but don't really like experiencing. If this is true then I would really love to be present with you; if it is not then I am sorry but I have been projecting something on to you'. You speak only from what you feel inside yourself. If you try to focus outside yourself to see what is going on in another person, that is always a projection and will always cause some sort of misunderstanding.

So if I feel it within me, that is seeing?

No, whatever you feel you feel inside of you. You never feel the outside; you experience everything inside yourself, including other people. But if you interpret the experience, it is not seeing anymore. If you have a feeling, or some sensation in the body, and you just meet that sensation without interpreting it, that is seeing. If you put a little story around it, you project your story onto the experience. There are external projections – and we can see these quite quickly – but there is also a lot of internal projecting happening. Either we project our story about an experience onto the experience as an interpretation or we project something onto ourselves; neither of these are seeing. Seeing is just the recognition of a movement within, and that very recognition is usually enough to see whether what is happening is just an old friend – a habitual reaction – or whether something new is happening. Seeing knows; you don't have to analyze what it knows. You know if the system is running down an old road. You don't have to know where it comes from or what it means, you just know that it is happening. That is seeing. Everything else is either an external projection or some interpretation about the experience you are having.

I feel that my mind wants a little formula to be able to understand, but I feel that actually I will simply have to know in every moment.

Yes, beautiful.

Nobody can give me a map.

Yes, you are mature, you are ever fresh, not standing on anything. You do not have a method or some technique you just repeat, because that has never worked. Sooner or later the technique turned against you. So it is just a matter of meeting our sensations ever freshly in every moment.

We only know what we know in the moment. It is a tremendous opportunity to meet your partner — even after you have known each other for years — ever freshly; to be ever fresh within, innocent, not carrying the burden of the past, the burden of stories and interpretations. Jiddu Krishnamurti described it as the freedom from the past.

The formula, the framework, the rules, whatever you want to call them, they just don't fit on me anymore.

Yes, I am happy to hear that. So now you have an opportunity to meet nakedly, without knowing. If we are present in order to change something, then it won't work. If we are present without any movement of wanting to change our actual experience, then that presence functions. When there is the slightest hidden agenda of shoulds and shouldn'ts, then it becomes a technique, and like any other technique it does not function. It is fortunate that it does not function, for then it can be an invitation to just have a very honest look inside yourself to see if there is any wanting to change your experience or to change the other person.

It's very subtle isn't it?

Very subtle. We love wanting to change. It is just very unfamiliar to us to allow the experience to be fully present. We love to believe in the promise that one day things will change. Somehow we have become used to following that hope. Some people give us the promise that if you follow them things will change, and the promise always ends up in disappointment. The one who gives the promise has a lot of stress because he knows he cannot meet that promise and the one who is following in the hope that there is going to be a change will soon be very disappointed. It's not about changing.

I am
not in
the world.

The whole
world is
in me.

Usually, with our mind and our senses, we try to meet the world from the inside out. There is a movement from within towards the world; to hear the world, to see the world, to understand the world as though it was 'out there'. In this movement it seems like the world is outside of us and this creates a sense of separation. If we allow that moving outwards to come to rest and allow the focus of attention to return to its own source — awareness — the whole world, the whole universe, is experienced as being within this awareness that is myself and yourself.

Being does not have attributes. It is without name, without form, it is no thing. It manifests as a wakeful passivity and gentle restfulness. It allows everything to be in it without any wanting to move towards a desired experience. It is non-doing; free of an inner reaction to experience and fully available for this moment.

I am desperately reading Ramana Maharshi's books at the moment but the words are not having the same impact they used to have.

Can you allow that to be, without any attempt to change it? And take an honest look: why do you read Ramana? What is the hidden agenda behind it? What do you want from him? If you are happy and everything is beautiful, do you read Ramana? When you are enjoying reality do you read Ramana? No. You are much happier enjoying the moment. What do you want from Ramana? As long as we want something from Ramana or whoever, are we happy unless we get it?

No.

And what about when reality changes in our experience and we believe it has to do with Ramana or somebody else?

Reading Ramana is good, but it is not the same as having my own direct experience of what he speaks about.

So what is the hidden agenda of the reading? I am speaking here of most reading, not all reading —

I have nothing against reading spiritual books. But what makes you read the book, what drives the activity? I am referring precisely to the experience you have just shared.

To make me feel better.

Yes. And the belief 'I had it and now I've lost it and I want to have it back' is resistance: not wanting to experience this moment as it is. Labelling our experience as pain or shame is interpretation. We interpret to give the experience a name, because we want to know what is going on. Can you have the experience you are having right now without any attempt to label it?

Yes.

How does that feel?

Good.

Even this 'good' can be an interpretation of the experience. We can speak in these terms, but even this labelling of something as good creates the possibility of bad.

I was looking for a word.

There is no word. Everything is an expression of that perfection that has no word.

So what do I do if I say something and it causes me to experience some contraction?

Experience the contraction.

If it is pain or shame?

Yes. It took me a while before I understood Jiddu Krishnamurti when he said 'Can you look at the tree without the name?'. What do you see when you look at me without labelling, without believing in any interpretation that might take place? What do you see?

Just you.

And where is the separation between you and me when you see just me? You won't find any. So we can say that when you see me, you also see yourself. You share yourself with yourself. I am speaking what you know, nothing added. When our interpretations are seen not to be true, we start afresh, we become humble again, to be a beginner every morning. To begin from the point of zero. To be much more or much less than 'being enlightened', to be much more or much less than 'I've got it'. This allows us to meet as ordinary people: the fun begins here. Whatever wants to be experienced and hasn't been met so far will show up. Whatever wants to come home, let it come. The quieter it gets inside, the less we are getting hooked. I am not interested in hope – that one day it is going to be better than this very moment. We can use Ramana's words to avoid truth and this is definitely not Ramana's teaching.

Take a nice glass of wine or a good beer – only a few people really enjoy it. Most drink the beer to not feel what they are feeling. I used to smoke a lot, and that smoking was not enjoyment; it was just not wanting to feel this very moment. The moment a feeling I did not like showed up I immediately took a cigarette. We are so used to avoiding and resisting feelings that anything can be turned into a tool to avoid reality: meditation, drinking, eating, smoking, reading, sex. Can you enjoy these things without wanting to avoid reality?

There is nothing 'wrong' with this avoidance of reality; we are just taking a clear look at how we are functioning. We are using our partners, our friends, our teachers, to avoid experiencing the moment very softly within ourselves. It's a huge thing to really see, and it is only because we believe in our interpretations.

The conditioning is so strong.

Is that thought the truth? Or an interpretation?

An interpretation.

What is the truth?

I don't know.

You don't know. Yes. So how strong is the conditioning when you don't interpret it?

There's nothing.

That's right. So if you would like to have strong conditioning, believe in the thought that the conditioning is strong.

It's like dust had collected and I swept it away.

Yes — beautiful. It's natural. You walk into a room after being away for a few days and there is dust on the table. We like it clean, so we dust the table, very naturally.

This dust is all our interpretations. If there is no interpretation, there is no wanting.

They go together.

The invitation is to investigate how the habit — and it is not your habit, it's an impersonal habit — of interpreting experience is linked to the focus of attention. The more the focus of attention is outwards, the more interpretation takes place.

So it's a matter of constant vigilance.

Yes, that is what you are. That vigilance, that wakefulness, that which sees and that which is already awake — infinite, ever-present, undisturbed wakefulness. You have never been asleep, you have just believed in your interpretations. That wakefulness is never affected by the interpretations.

Sometimes reality can be too much.

Is this moment too much?

No.

Can reality ever be too much? If we believe it can ever be too much, we believe that God makes mistakes and that we know better.

So let us see how this feeling that reality can be too much is generated, because sometimes we do have the feeling 'Oh, this is too much'.

Maybe we don't have to talk about it. I can stand it.

This is an avoidance you are very used to, and it actually has served you for quite a long time. It was helpful, we can say. But now that very 'I can stand it' can very easily turn into a hardness on yourself. Actually it has always been a hardness and that hardness is a very subtle form of resistance that makes us not move, but inside it is really hard and uncomfortable.

It is getting softer.

So it is not about standing something. It is about letting that experience that is present be very softly here. The experience will not change, but the way you are meeting this experience changes. That's the name of the game. Really to allow yourself to be here amidst this very moment. Moving away would be another form of resistance.

If you go from here to there, you will experience the same thing there. There is no escape from reality. We cannot escape life; wherever we go, we take ourselves with us, fully. That's the beauty of it. In this very moment, can there be anything too much when we are just that very softness? Have a look. From the perspective of 'standing it' and being hard, sometimes it seems too much, but that feeling of too much is generated by the hardness, and through a hard discipline we 'stand it'.

Or fear.

Or fear, or whatever. But can you see that this feeling 'this is too much' is generated by that hardness, that tightening up? The moment you become soft in the same situation is it still too much? And be very honest. In that very moment is it too much?

No.

So that very sense of too much can actually be a very beautiful invitation to you – just to feel where there is hardness in you and to meet that hardness with softness.

They are already dancing with each other.

Yes, they are beginning to love each other. It is a profound understanding to see that nothing can be too much, otherwise it would not be. How can this moment be too much? If it was too much it would not be this moment.

For me I cannot see this every single moment.

There is no every single moment. There is only ever this moment. Moment, moment, moment; only the moment.

This moment is perfect; and we can realize that perfection not by changing something on the outside or by looking for another moment, but by seeing that very softness within as perfection. Being soft with the moment is perfection, is love.

Not wanting to be in the body is a big trap of spiritual seekers around the world. It is a belief in the promise that 'there' is better than here. Not wanting to experience certain sensations is not wanting to be fully embodied. You are in the body, and you will be in the body as long as God wants you to be. The body is not a prison: the prison is the wanting to get out of it. Freedom is to be fully embodied.

To be fully embodied is the opportunity to experience consciousness fully without any sense of separation and to experience that here and now. Only when we believe that there are some sensations we do not want to experience does it seem that there is a separation between inside and outside. To be fully in the body and experience all sensations – even if they are unpleasant sometimes – is the key to living as consciousness here and now.

The body is a tremendous gift, a gift that enables us to be here. The mind can be somewhere else and the affections can be somewhere else, but the body can only be here, every moment of our lives.

I always seem to project my thoughts into the past or the future. I will replay things that have happened in the past, either exactly as I remember or trying to change things I could have said better or that could have turned out better. When I am in an argument with someone I may not know what to say, but an hour later I will think of something I really should have said to cut the other person down. Or I may project into the future — what I am going to do, what others are going to do and things like that; trying to play out things that haven't happened yet.

Have you heard the story of the man who wanted to borrow a hammer? One day he needs a hammer, but he hasn't got one, so he has the idea to ask the man who lives next door. But as he has never met his neighbor before he is quite shy about going to ask. So he starts thinking about how he is going to ask the neighbor. He thinks if he goes and rings the bell he might disturb him. He imagines the neighbor saying to him 'You disturbed me.' So the man starts thinking what he is going to say in reply. He goes over in his mind the most suitable ways to apologize to the neighbor. Then he starts thinking that maybe he might be very unfriendly with me even if I apologize for disturbing him. So he then starts thinking about what he is going to say if the neighbor is unfriendly. By now he is getting quite upset. 'Maybe he will call me an idiot for not owning a simple thing like a hammer,' the man begins to fear. 'I will not allow that,' he thinks. He gets more and more angry as he reflects on this insult to his intelligence. In a fit of rage he goes round to the neighbor's house and bangs on the front door. As the neighbor answers, he shouts at the man 'You bastard. You are the rudest neighbor I have ever known. You can stuff your bloody hammer. I wouldn't want to borrow it if it was the last bloody hammer on earth'.

Something like that just played out for me. It's so funny.

How does it feel to see this pattern, this old friend; to just be aware of this pattern, whatever it is?

It's kind of fun, kind of a game.

Yes. The moment we believe in our patterns we act like the guy going round to his neighbor's door, believing what we have imagined is already reality, and we act like a fool. So, instead, can we enjoy those patterns? This is a profound question. Usually we like to be at peace and we don't like to experience patterns that don't feel good, so the moment a pattern shows up, there is a mechanism of not wanting to have this experience and we will use anything available to try to get rid of it. We grew up being told we had to function well, feel good and be nice people, so whenever an unpleasant feeling comes up we try to suppress it. If we believe that a pattern does anything to us or that it means something about us – for example that I am a bad person – this is just an interpretation, and when we believe that interpretation we are almost fully involved.

But what if a pattern is operating in me and I don't realize it and I think I'm free?

That itself is a pattern. If you start worrying about patterns you are not aware of, that is a pattern. You are like the man worrying about what his neighbor's reaction to him will be before he is aware of it. It can happen that a pattern plays out, and somehow we know it is operating, but we cannot see the pattern itself or a way out of it. When this happens, we can meet it by being gentle with the reality that we will become aware of it only when we become aware of it; not one second before and not one second after. It will happen in the moment when it will happen, and it is not in our hands. How does that feel?

Peaceful.

This is true peace, if we can live as peace in the midst of any circumstance. Whatever happens, we are that peace. That very awareness that is present now; its nature is peace. It is not at peace; it is peace. There is a huge difference. Being at peace means that we still believe we can do something to be at peace, or that it requires certain circum- stances to be at peace. Being the peace does not depend on anything; it is prior to, underlies and remains after every experience.

Every cell in your body
transmits information
about how you are inside
and receives information about
how others are inside.
There is a constant exchange
of information about being.
Just let this touch you,
not trying to change anything.

Being a spiritual person is opposed to being awake. Being a spiritual person is just an identity like any other, and all identities are a protection of the heart, an avoidance of living nakedly. To live nakedly is to be open to what is and not superimpose on reality the identity of a spiritual person, or any other identity. The heart, to protect itself, has used everything including beingness and spirituality. To be completely available for what is includes being available for your heart to be closed when it is closed and not trying to open it.

For the heart to be truly open it must first break. An open heart is the fruit of that availability to let everything, including everything in us, be as it is however much we may want it to be otherwise. The reality is we do not open the heart; it opens in the breaking when we give up protecting it.

Softly give up the protection of the heart whenever you see it operating. Do not be hard on yourself; this is another protection of the heart from the pain of breaking. How can the heart break, how can the heart open, when you are hard on yourself? It cannot.

At one point in my life I learned that my mother had not wanted me to be born, and on the day I found out I felt like I did not exist.

But even though your mother did not want you, you are still here. No problem. And you don't even know if she didn't want you or if she was afraid of the pain.

She was afraid of staying together with my father.

That may be. What does it have to do with you?

Nothing.

Nothing. You are here.

But it has influenced all my life up to now.

What has influenced your life is that you believed in the thought 'my mother did not want to have me'. You believed in that thought so much that you thought it was the truth. This is an inner projection. If somebody gives you feedback and you believe he is right, this is an outer projection. If a thought pops up, maybe together with a feeling, and you believe that thought, then it is an inner projection. There are outer projections, and the same mechanism can happen inwardly; you project it onto yourself. Every projection ends up with an interpretation and this interpretation always turns into a judgement about ourself. So if somebody says 'I love you' and you believe that, it is quickly turned into 'I am lovable'. Everything, positive or negative, when we speak in those terms is a projection that quickly turns into a self-centered judgement: I am loved or I am not loved; I am great or I am very small. That is just the second step after believing in those projections.

There are so many projections.

In all of us; it is very beautiful that you see that. That seeing and that honesty is the dropping, is the letting go of it. Not changing it; just seeing that tremendous mechanism of projecting or taking projections and not believing that our projections or those of others are the truth. If we believe them, we are caught. Don't *try* to drop them. That very seeing and not believing is the dropping. This morning in yoga the question came 'what am I doing here?'. And there was no possibility of believing this question, because it did not make any sense, and it dropped. The heaviness in this question, that subtle feeling of not being at ease, contained a fantasy option; that the moment could be different from what it was. That is the nature of the question 'what am I doing here?'. Does the truth that you are need a good feeling?

No, it's nice but it's not necessary.

Beautiful description – beautiful. So who is the master; you or your mind?

I am.

Allow yourself that unfamiliar sense. Some natural authority comes back to you. It's not about 'being someone', it's about that natural authority; call it freedom or love or strength. Let that natural freedom come home. For as long as we believe our projections, we also project the freedom outside. Be the freedom without interpreting it. Sometimes it feels difficult, sometimes it feels lovely, but that doesn't change the certainty. Freedom has no meaning. It needs nothing to confirm it.

Don't try to not want; that is also wanting. Just rest as that beauty; that enjoyment. Then that enjoyment is enough in itself; you don't need to grab anything.

I invite you as the freedom shows up to embrace the beauty and the possibilities of this world in that freedom: watching football, drinking a good beer, playing with friends – all this normal, ordinary stuff. It took me a while to get back to enjoying these simple things again. During a silent retreat something shifted. I don't know what it was but I felt very light. Then one night I went to the Ramana ashram and entered the main gate, which I had always enjoyed. I went in, and suddenly I felt such a weight and burden on my shoulders – really physically – seeing all those serious seekers. It did not have to do with them or the ashram; I just had this feeling of being under a gravestone. I did not know why, but I felt it. I went home and felt light again. It was a very deep release of some old stuff, some 'spiritual' weight that had still been on my shoulders. Ramana now seems to be much more a friend inside than outside and I can enjoy being ordinary again.

Last night a very painful insecurity was coming up in me, a very old feeling of profound insecurity. And I saw how I believed in the movie around me; how when the movie says I am lovable I feel lovable and if the movie says that I'm not — if I am with my partner and he is not being affectionate to me — then I am not lovable.

Beautiful.

There was this pain and then the beautiful thing was a voice deep within me that said 'I am with you through this no matter what. No matter how painful it gets, no matter how long, I will be here with you'.

In India they refer to this as the Inner Guru, this inner intelligence. I don't like the word guru — it is that inner intelligence that is with you all the time. It is that awareness. That awareness is the master, the real master. Only when we project the awareness outside does it appear as an external master. But that awareness is the inner master. It is beautiful what you speak of. That awareness is the true master.

And that love can only come from within.

Beautiful.

(Laughing) And then I get mad at the movie because it won't give me love!

Yes. If you go into a cinema and see a beautiful love scene, a beautiful face saying 'I love you', would you believe that? Would you believe this big picture on the screen saying 'I love you'?

It's just a movie.

Yes, it's just a movie. You would say 'Oh, a beautiful scene, and very beautifully acted – very authentic, a lot of emotion involved'. But you would never believe that it has something to do with you. When this person was playing this scene, he was certainly not thinking about you. He only had his script and his director telling him what to do. It is beautiful how clearly you see.

Can you meet emotional pain without wanting someone else to hold you? Can you meet it without trying to change it; not trying to be warm when it's cold, or joyful when there's pain, but just meeting it the way it is, with nothing between?

Most of us have the habit of creating pictures, of imagining nice pictures when reality is not nice. So as long as we believe the picture and say 'I'm fine', 'everything is beautiful', 'everything is love', 'nothing is wrong', 'I do not feel any pain' we are hypnotized by the self-created picture and we are not present. But when the picture is dropped a true meeting with reality and with others can be made.

Truth is not interested in personality. Personality is not able to speak truth. Beyond personality is that which can be expressed without being affected by the personality. Is the truth that you are still encapsulated by the personality? The personality is not meant to be a stop to life taking over. In fact, it is not really a stop; it is just a habit. If it were truly a stop it would mean that the personality is stronger than truth or love, and it isn't. It may delay life taking over, but in the end it cannot stop it.

In waking up, there is synchronicity. The wakefulness of the true being penetrates every layer of the personality in each moment. Then there is one: it is not truth versus personality. It is one. The personality then functions in a different way; things come to peace that have not been at peace before, and the truth that was caged is set free like a flying bird.

There are things that happened in the past between my son and his father that my son now wants to deal with in a particular way. He is an adult and I know I have to respect his choices and decisions, but if he goes forward on his present course it will cause a lot of pain for everyone.

What we usually do is try to change the outside, or others, in order not to feel something in ourselves. One possibility – when we have heard about beingness – is that we say to ourselves we will 'let him be'. But, again, this is not really letting be; it is a very subtle form of resistance. We protect the heart with it because we do not know how to respond to the situation. But we constantly feel what is going on in those we are close to, so it doesn't work. The other possibility is that we start 'helping' the other person. We start thinking about what we can do for him and her. We become doers with good intentions and screw things up. So neither way works – they are both avoidance of feeling what is going on in you.

So can you meet what is touched in you when you look at your son the way he is – with all the destruction it may cause and the rest of it? Can you look your son without either denying what you heart is saying or wanting to change him? Can you look at him without taking anything on your shoulders, while inviting him with all his pain to be felt in you? Your son and you are not separate at the level of the heart. There is only one, and that is the sensation that is here, now. Denying something in him denies something in you and denying something in you denies something in him.

Our families are the ground in which we are rooted. I have seen many people go on spiritual retreat in India and then break with their families; and they are not grounded. They think they are more enlightened and free, but I do not see any happiness in them. The more you include all of your family, and all that they are, the more awake you are.

I feel a sense of 'I am' and a connectedness with others, but from another viewpoint it cannot really be described as connectedness.

Yes, I sense that in you. The feeling of oneness with every being on earth can only happen when there is a very gentle and tender inquiry into the way we are protecting our heart. I can remember being in the midst of a group of people and I felt not the slightest connection to anyone, and yet there was a feeling of 'I am'. It was a subtle tendency of protecting the heart, of not wanting to drop the little distance I was keeping between myself and others – of not wanting to experience everything in me and everything in them.

We can never feel deeper in another than we can feel in ourselves. There are places in all of us that are unknown territory. We know where we feel safe and we know where we do not feel safe. The moment we meet something unknown, our system kicks in to protect us from it. The system lets it be. But this is not the true letting be; it is letting what has been asleep in us remain asleep. The system says 'I am' but this is not the true 'I am'. It is not complete. There is a little movement away from fully meeting something in us. The more we gently discover those places in us that have not completely woken up, and the more we feel safe with those places in us, the deeper we can experience connectedness.

These places do not bother us while they are sleeping, but every so often they are touched, and then a shutting down happens. When we are not safe with those places in ourselves, we most of the time feel a sense of insecurity when we meet people for whom these places are also not safe. This way, life becomes a very limited experience; we can only connect with particular people. We may see others, but we cannot really connect with them. We live a fragmented life. The good news is that only as awareness can we meet these unfamiliar places in us.

The feeling of 'I am' that you described is not the end but the beginning of the capacity to meet yourself and to feel safe in yourself in places that are unknown. And whenever you can feel safe in places that have been asleep in you, the ability to meet others in those places expands dramatically.

What is real in you is not
known by the mind.

If you live as awareness
the mind is always behind,
until it merges with awareness.

Do not fight the mind.
Allow it to come home to
awareness.

And then the limited mind
becomes the infinite mind.

Right now I have only one question that seems worth asking. How can I live as the love that I am?

(Voice breaks up and the eyes fill with tears)

You are the answer. Just that breaking of the heart is the answer.

What comes to mind is one simple thing about that beautiful question. That question is one of only a few that are not to be answered. And these are the best questions.

Just let your life be a fresh and direct response to that question from moment to moment. That is the way I deal with that question, because I have the same question in my heart. I have not found an answer and I am not looking for an answer, but that question moves me. It is not that I deal with the question, but that the question deals with me. This way I become an instrument for the question. There is nothing to hold on to. Only love can ask this question, because only love is interested in being itself.

That very core that you are is asking this question.

Love asks 'How can I live as my own self'. For me it is one of the most beautiful questions a human being can ask, and one of the most courageous.

This question is a gateway, so that the very love it speaks of is lived in our daily life and is not converted into a dead philosophy. It is an actual reality every moment of life, wherever we are. It is not to be made a big thing of. It is a subtle sweetness that does not impose itself on others but which others catch the fragrance of.

In that love affair, in that fire of love, wherever that consciousness sees some hardness in myself — which shows up as some tightening of the body — that very seeing, and being soft with that tightening up, is a deepening of that love affair.

Every time a softening happens, and sometimes it is a miracle that it happens, it seems that the capacity of the system to be love expands. It is nothing that we do; it is just the fruit that we are given by being loving and being soft within.

My experience is that this can happen for a few days, but not over a longer period.

It is the beginning of that love affair. My invitation, my joy that I share with you, is whenever that consciousness, that very self – you – sees any tightening up, just give yourself time and let that love meet that hardness and let it return to softness. It will make a huge difference in your life and to everyone you meet in your life.

I have come to learn not to interfere with how love expresses itself. There were still some images in me about how that love should be, how that love should express itself in my life. It took a while to drop those images. The greatest challenge to let that question move for me has been in my partnership, because in our intimate partnerships we are more vulnerable than anywhere else. Every single place inside that we do not want to experience will show up and every protection of the heart will also show up. Every resistance, every not wanting to be present with our own experience, comes up. That is the beauty of a sincere partnership, a committed partnership. To be love in a beautiful environment is a piece of cake. To live as love in the midst of struggle, pain or blame is where the dark places inside show up.

I was touched by the words 'How can I live as love?'.

Yes, and it is not about having love or giving love; it is about being love. Love is our true nature and so we do not really need to speak about it. What can be of value is to speak about are the ways in which we are not living as love, the ways in which we are not ourselves.

What puzzles me is the difference between a discipline and being that question.

This is a very good question. So from the perspective of what has been revealed to you so far, how would you answer that? How does that touch of the heart that gives you a glimpse of your true nature answer?

A discipline needs an individual who needs to accomplish something. But without discipline it is difficult for me to stay with the wisdom.

If you stay with the wisdom, are you the wisdom or is it separate from you? When you talk in terms of having to stay with the wisdom, you separate yourself from it. Can you ever lose what you are?

No, but I can jump into believing something else and it is so painful when I do.

Now feel the pain that you put on the pain; the pain of beating yourself up when the natural pain of separation is experienced. What do you expect from being so hard in yourself? Does it work?

No.

When we put things on our shoulders about the way we think we should be, we cut ourselves off from others. We lose innocence in the moment we take on a point of view. Live what is true now to your own heart.

The maturing of the heart is not something that you can speed up artificially by the imposition of a discipline from outside: discipline can be just another way of protecting the heart. When we protect the heart we become separated from our experience. We go into the head where the touch of the heart cannot function. It is the breaking of the heart that transforms. This is the way we are purified, not by the pain of being hard on ourselves.

MORE FROM FLORIAN SCHLOSSER

For details of public meetings and silent retreats with Florian Schlosser, plus CDs and DVDs, visit www.tathagata.de and shop.tathagata.de.

CONSCIOUS.TV

Conscious.tv is a TV channel broadcasting on the Internet at www.conscious.tv. Certain programmes are also broadcast on Satellite TV stations based in the UK. The channel aims to stimulate debate, question, enquire, inform, enlighten, encourage and inspire people in the areas of Consciousness, Healing and Psychology.

CONSCIOUS.TV and NON-DUALITY PRESS
present two unique DVD releases

CONVERSATIONS ON NON-DUALITY
VOLUME 1

Tony Parsons — *The Open Secret* • Rupert Spira — *The Transparency of Things* — Parts 1 & 2 • Richard Lang — *Seeing Who You Really Are*

CONVERSATIONS ON NON-DUALITY
VOLUME 2

Jeff Foster — *Life Without a Centre* • Richard Sylvester — *I Hope You Die Soon* • Roger Linden — *The Elusive Obvious*

Available to order from:
www.non-dualitypress.com

Breinigsville, PA USA
20 September 2010
245736BV00002B/22/P